WHAT
THE RAF AIRMAN
TOOK TO WAR

Bill Howard

Photographs by Michael H. Wagner

Foreword by Squadron Leader Geoffrey Wellum DFC

SHIRE PUBLICATIONS

Published in Great Britain in 2015 by Shire Publications Ltd (part of
Bloomsbury Publishing Plc) PO Box 883, Oxford, OX1 9PL, UK.
PO Box 3985, New York, NY 10185-3985, USA.

E-mail: shire@shirebooks.co.uk   www.shirebooks.co.uk

A CIP catalogue record for this book is available from the British Library.

Shire General no. 11.   ISBN-13: 978 1 78442 055 0
PDF e-book ISBN: 978 1 78442 078 9
ePub ISBN: 978 1 78442 077 2

Bill Howard has asserted his right under the Copyright, Designs and Patents
Act, 1988, to be identified as the author of this book.

Typeset in Garamond, Perpetua and Gill Sans.
Printed in China through Worldprint Ltd.

15 16 17 18 19   10 9 8 7 6 5 4 3 2 1

DEDICATION

7543

For my parents, William G. and Laura Howard, and for Katie in London.

ACKNOWLEDGEMENTS
The author would like to thank
all those who have supported the
publication of this volume, with
special appreciation to Russell
Butcher and Shire Publications
and Michael H. Wagner (www.
PerceptibleDesign.com), who
created some stunning photographs
for this project. Great thanks also
to Paulette Morgan, and to Peter
Elliott of the RAF Museum in
Hendon. Much gratitude is due to
Squadron Leader Geoffrey Wellum
DFC, a veteran of the Battle of
Britain, who wrote the foreword
to this volume. I also thank Nigel
Flitter and Mike Moffitt for access
to items from their collections, as
well as the Imperial War Museum
and the Australian War Memorial. I
was honoured to have known Wing
Commander Gordon L. Sinclair.
He is remembered in these pages.

IMAGE CREDITS
Australian War Memorial, page 64;
Nigel Flitter Collection, pages 62,
83; Imperial War Museum, page
66; Mike Moffitt Collection, page
90. All other images belong to Bill
Howard and Michael H. Wagner.

CONTENTS

FOREWORD BY SQUADRON LEADER GEOFFREY WELLUM DFC

Seventy-five years ago, a small band of pilots took to the skies above Britain to defend against the real peril of German invasion. These pilots turned back that tide and handed Germany its first defeat in the Second World War. It was, however, a very near thing. Nevertheless, the Germans realised that they had suffered their first significant defeat and been denied their aim, and they did not like it.

Those exciting days are distant now, but in the pages of this book, one can remember those who gave so much in defence of England during that terrible summer of 1940. Most of my fellow pilots who fought in the Battle of Britain are gone now. The passing years have thinned our proud ranks and taken away almost all of those who flew during those four crucial months in 1940. Although they are gone, I remember my friends and comrades who each gave so much to defend England.

In these pages the reader can see the tunics that were worn, the flying equipment that was used and the things that were carried by the nearly 3,000 pilots and aircrew who will forever be remembered as 'The Few'.

Geoffrey Wellum

THE RAF AT WAR

Much has been written about the pilots who served in the Royal Air Force (RAF) during the Second World War. While 'The Few' were recognised as the saviours of England even as the bombs fell, Great Britain successfully resisted the German attacks with a national response. The latter included the commitment of pilots of the RAF Fighter, Bomber and Coastal commands, the Royal Navy, as well as that of the people of England.

Because of the romantic image of the fighter pilot, RAF aviators captured much of the glory in the war's early days – they provided an inspiring example. But although the pilots gained much of the credit for victory in what became known as the Battle of Britain, it is a legacy that has been challenged in recent years. Some historians have given credit to the Royal Navy for dissuading Hitler from invading Britain, while others have argued that the Battle of Britain was won not so much by 'The Few', but by the many – the tenacious British citizenry who were determined to see that democracy would continue in Europe even as the Axis forces conquered one country after another from 1939 to 1940.

Hurricane fighters of No. 242 Squadron at Duxford. This Hurricane crashed on 28 March 1941, killing its pilot, Arthur William Smith.

The everyday heroism displayed by the people of Great Britain was inspired and sustained by the brave example exhibited by the RAF. Whether British born or as refugees from nations already conquered by the Axis forces, RAF pilots were motivated to engage the enemy for a variety of reasons. Some were determined to defend their homeland, while the Belgian, French, Czech and Polish RAF pilots sought to avenge what had already been inflicted upon their nations, and to try to turn the tide of fortune. American, Canadian and Commonwealth nation pilots saw what was happening over Britain as a battleground for democracy and understood that if the Axis powers were not defeated, the war would expand. Regardless of national identity or individual motivation, RAF pilots fought with fierce tenacity.

A German Bf 109E-1, downed near Lewes in August 1940. Unterofficer Leo Zaunbrecher survived the crash and was captured.

There was a great deal of stress inherent in the operations. Pilots were awakened to begin a day's work that would not end until sunset. Transported out to the airfields, they would wait for the 'scramble' call in full kit, playing card games or reading newspapers to pass the time. When the telephone rang, the pilots would sprint to their planes and be strapped into their seats. The fighters would rumble down grassy runways to gain speed for take-off. Once in the air, just a few minutes of combat could exhaust a pilot flying at 30,000 feet in an unpressurised aircraft. The noise of battle and the

RAF pilots re-enacting a 'scramble' in 1946. Note the pilot (second left) carrying a squadron dog in his arms.

roar of engines pounded on eardrums and the G-forces associated with the violent twists and turns of dogfighting brought the pilots to the verge of blacking out. They needed to focus all of their energy and concentration on flying while their body endured incredible physical forces. Every pilot knew the dangers of combat flying – they had lost friends and comrades in fiery crashes or seen young lives ruined by wounds and the disfigurement caused by burning cockpits. War took its toll on these young men every day.

Pilot Officer Peter Parrott remembered: 'once you were in action, you were too busy trying to shoot something down or trying not to be shot down yourself to be frightened.' Pilot Officer John Ellacombe recalled:

[T]here were fourteen, fifteen hours of daylight each day. You were on duty right through. Chaps were being lost all the time. We had seventeen out of twenty-three killed or wounded in my squadron in less than three weeks. We had another eight aircraft shot down with the chaps unhurt, including myself twice. It was a fight for survival. There was a tremendous 'twitch'. If somebody slammed a door, half the chaps would jump out of their chairs. There were times when you were so tired, you'd pick up your pint of beer with two hands. But no one was cowering, terrified in a corner. My greatest fear was that I'd reach the stage where I'd show fear. But it took me years after the war to get rid of my twitch.

John Ellacombe
joined the RAF in
1939 and served in
No. 151 Squadron.

Those who served during the Battle of Britain never forgot the experience. It was, for most, the central moment of their lives. Although many went on to serve in other places during the war, the experiences of 1940 coloured every hour and made forgetting the war experience very difficult. In 1972, a historian wrote to the pilot Ronald 'Ras' Berry of No. 603 Squadron requesting information about 'his most memorable victory' during the Battle of Britain. Berry bluntly responded: 'My most memorable victory was waking up for another day having survived the day before.' Pilot Christopher Foxley-Norris recalled:

> I still don't like the telephone because you'd be sitting there in the dispersal hut, playing cards or reading a book or something like that, and the telephone would ring. Everyone froze. An orderly answered. It might be 'Squadron scramble' or something quite unimportant … But the tension which built up between the ringing of the phone and learning what it was is my hangover from the Battle of Britain. I still don't like telephones.

In such simple things was the line between the relatively peaceful life on the ground and the violent confrontations that took place in the sky. It was a daily tension. Richard Hillary, a pilot who did not survive the war, described it as 'moments of great boredom interspersed with moments of great excitement.'

Ronald 'Ras' Berry
during the Battle of
Britain.

It is easy to romanticise the pilots who fought in the Battle of Britain as larger-than-life characters – the stuff of legend. What the celebrated 'Few' accomplished during the course of just a few months in 1940 was inspiring. Had Britain failed in 1940, the war would have progressed very differently for the Allies. It is remarkable to consider how much rested on the shoulders of the young RAF fighter pilots whose average age fell between just nineteen and twenty-four.

Undated photo of Polish RAF pilots in the dispersal hut awaiting orders, their Mae West jackets partially inflated in readiness for action.

RAF pilots relaxing at Tangmere in February 1941. Four of the six pictured did not survive the war.

The timeframe for the Battle of Britain period was defined as 10 July to 31 October 1940. These dates were used to determine eligibility for the Battle of Britain clasp, which is worn as an attachment on the 1939–45 Star medal, and is accompanied by a silver gilt rosette sewn to the ribbon bar. Only those who flew operationally during the 114 days

of recognised battle duration qualify to be considered as one of 'The Few'.

Fewer than 3,000 pilots were awarded the Battle of Britain clasp. Most of these (2,334 to be precise) were British born. Non-British aircrews totalled 583 men, of which Poles were the largest contingent (145) followed by New Zealanders (126), Canadians (98) and Czechs (88). Australia provided 33 aircrew, with Belgium (29), South Africa (25), Free France (13) and the United States (9) supplying the rest. The Olympian Billy Fiske of No. 601 Squadron was the first American to be killed in RAF service during the Second World War. He died on 17 August 1940, one day after being critically wounded during a dogfight.

Roughly half of those who earned the Battle of Britain clasp were commissioned officers and many who survived the battle went on to attain higher rank in the RAF. About 42 per cent of the Battle of Britain pilots were non-commissioned officers (NCOs). These men flew fighters but also served as aircrew in other planes such as Boulton Paul Defiants, Bristol Beaufighters or Bristol Blenheims. Those NCOs who qualified for the clasp included warrant officers, flight sergeants, sergeants and even corporals and aircraftmen. Women who served in the Women's Auxiliary Air Force (WAAF) performed admirably and were essential to flight operations, but were never made eligible to wear the Battle of Britain clasp.

Royal Canadian Air Force (RCAF) pilots, B. F. Christmas (left) and W. P. Sprenger in 1940. Sprenger was killed on 26 November 1940.

Casualty figures for the Battle of Britain lack consistency. One study reports that 544 aircrew lost their lives in the battle. The Air Ministry claimed 375 killed and 358 wounded, while recent historians have identified 443 killed. The numbers translate into about thirty-three RAF pilots killed each week – or five men per day. Commissioned

officers accounted for 62 per cent of the losses. About 38 per cent (193) were NCOs. Of 'The Few' who continued fighting after 1940, 795 had lost their lives by 1945. Of the 2,917 men who made up 'The Few', 45.9 per cent (1,339) did not survive the war. The RAF recognises 814 of 'The Few' who died in subsequent operations.

After the war, 'The Few' were commemorated with fly-past ceremonies, receptions, monument dedications and in hundreds of published historical accounts. As time passed, the retelling of the stories made the men who fought for the RAF seem larger than life. In the popular story of the battle, its veterans were like the knights of old England. They were a small and elite band of brothers joined together in common purpose against the enemy. It was an image that many of the pilots embraced and may have been part of the coping mechanisms they applied to the grim fighting days of their youth. The odds were against them – both personally and for Britain. What kept them going was an understanding that what they were fighting for was better than the cause of their enemy. A failure to succeed in their mission would have had grave implications for the world.

Yet in all this adoration, something was lost – a chapter hidden from popular understanding. The RAF pilot Brian Kingcome, of No. 92 Squadron, questioned in his memoir published in 1999: 'Why can't they just talk about Battle of

RAF pilots resting in front of their Spitfires at Biggin Hill late in the war. Ground crew are at work in the background.

19

Britain pilots? Why does it always have to be heroes? I think it devalues the word and denigrates all those who were called on to face just as great odds.' Indeed, not every RAF pilot flew in the Battle of Britain and the RAF's different forces – Fighter, Bomber, and Coastal commands – were active in all theatres during the Second World War, including North Africa, the Middle East and the South Pacific – and some were even stationed in North America. The RAF was a multinational force that defended many nations during the war. Its intelligence officers helped to crack secret German codes, and the WAAF provided essential support to air operations.

The RAF personnel of 1939–45 were men of flesh and blood who gave all that they could give for victory. This book is a reminder that while what they achieved was remarkable, they were ordinary people facing a common challenge. During the Second World War, the fate of the free world rested in their hands. The uniforms they wore, the medals they earned and the things they carried to war are reminders that connect us to them long after their deeds have become history. These pilots understood that if fighting for their country was not enough, they were risking their lives for something that was even greater than that. As Hitler's forces rumbled across Europe and a third of the world fell under his regime, it was the RAF that helped to resist that advance.

WHAT
THE RAF AIRMAN
TOOK TO WAR

RAF MOTTO

The motto of the Royal Air Force dates back to 1912, and to the early days of the Royal Flying Corps (RFC). The first commanding officer of the RFC was Colonel Frederick Sykes, who directed his officers to come up with an appropriate motto for the new air branch.

According to RAF legend, shortly after the assignment was given, two junior flying officers were discussing ideas about the motto. One of them, Lieutenant J. S. Yule, mentioned the phrase 'Per Ardua ad Astra', which he translated as 'Through Struggles to the Stars'. Yule had read a book entitled *The People of the Mist* by H. Rider Haggard, who had seen the phrase inscribed on some stone columns supporting the gates that led to a grand African estate. Colonel Sykes approved the proposed motto and forwarded it to the War Office. It was then submitted to King George V, who approved its adoption on 15 March 1913. The motto was subsequently adopted by the RAF on its formation in 1918.

A precise translation of the motto is in question. There have been a number of meanings ascribed to 'Ardua' and 'Astra' and scholars have declared the words untranslatable. The RAF and Commonwealth Air Forces have ignored the linguistic debate and 'Through Adversity to the Stars' has been the RAF's proud motto over the course of two world wars and through numerous conflicts to the present day.

Adventure in the skies!

AIR CREW QUALIFICATIONS

PILOTS   Age: over 18 under 31 | Education; Junior

RECRUITMENT

The average age of an RAF pilot in 1940 was about twenty. Some were as young as eighteen and there were others over thirty. Granted that the age of majority was set at twenty-one in 1940, many of the RAF's Battle of Britain pilots were not old enough to vote at a time when they risked their lives in battle every day.

Given the prevailing romantic image of the fighter pilot, the RAF had less difficulty than other branches of the armed forces in securing volunteers. Those who had grown up reading of the heroic fighter aces of the Great War needed little additional inspiration to find the RAF an attractive option for war service.

The adoption of the National Service Act required all able-bodied males to engage in war work. Many of the young men who had heard stories of the trench war of 1914–18 viewed the RAF as a better option for service. After volunteering, applicants would return to their civilian occupations until receiving a joining letter. Volunteers would then report to an Air Crew Reception Centre for medical examination, training and processing. One RAF recruit recalled that only about one in ten of the volunteers who reported were accepted into RAF service.

In 1940 a pilot officer could expect to earn £264 per annum, and NCOs quite a bit less, despite facing the same dangers; both received an allowance (flying pay) recognising their aircrew status. In addition, RAF numbers were strengthened in 1939 by pilots from the Auxiliary Air Force (AAF), who provided a civilian pool of extra capability during emergencies.

Other sources of manpower were the University Air Squadrons, created to attract young talent to the service, and the RAF Volunteer Reserve (RAFVR).

GROUND CREW

While pilots were celebrated as heroes, it was ground crew who made sure the planes were properly fuelled and maintained. In 1939, the RAF counted a ground crew force of slightly more than 100,000; by 1945, that number had increased to nearly 690,000. The slang term used to refer to non-commissioned airmen below the rank of corporal was 'Erks', but this was used as a term of affection rather than derision and had a long history within the RAF. Ground crew accepted the nickname. Those who enlisted in the RAF or the WAAF aged eighteen or older were allocated to one of six trade group classifications. Each classification reflected a particular skill or duty. The three lowest grades were Aircraftman (or Airwoman) 2nd Class, Aircraftman (or Airwoman) 1st Class and Leading Aircraftman (or Airwoman). Considering the grade system, the lowest true rank in ground crew was corporal, escalating in rank to sergeant, flight sergeant and warrant officer. Promotion to higher rank was sometimes made by station commanders on a temporary basis to fill vacancies, but only the RAF Records Office could formally make promotions. However essential the 'Erks' were, there was class separation between pilots and ground crew. In his book *No Moon Tonight*, former Bomber Command navigator Don Charlwood recalled a ground crew airman 'having an accent which left him safe from RAF commissioning.' The photograph opposite depicts an array of items including an other ranks wool forage cap and Air Ministry tools recovered from a wartime airfield. The photograph on the left shows Czech ground crew at Duxford in 1940, while the image on the right shows ground crew surrounding the Tempest flown by the New Zealand RAF pilot James Sheddan of No. 485 Squadron.

George the Sixth

... Britain, Ireland and the British Dominions

... the Faith, Emperor of India. To

... ty and well beloved   Reginald

... ecial Trust and Confidence in your Loyalty Courage

... titute and Appoint you to be an Officer in Our Active

... on the   Thirtieth   day of   May   1940

... to discharge your Duty as such in the Rank of

... as He may from time to time hereafter be pleased to

... tion will be made in the Canada Gazette or in such other manner as may for

... same being to preserved by Us in Council, and you are in such manner and

... be presented by Us to exercise and well discipline in Arms, both the infer...

... serving under you and use your best endeavours to keep them in good

... and them to Obey you as their superior Officer

... Directions as from time to time you shall receive

... ng to the Rules and Discipline of War in pursua...

In Witness Whereof Our Governor General of Ca...
... hereunto set his hand and Seal at Our Government Hou...
... the Thirtieth   day of   July   in the Year of Ou...
... Nine Hundred and   Forty   and in the
... Year of Our Reign
By Command of His Excellency th...

Air Secretary for   Ministe...

OFFICER'S COMMISSION

The aircrew who served in the RAF were all volunteers. After selection for pilot training, prospective pilots were subject to intense evaluation and examination to determine their suitability for flight operations. The time taken to qualify as a pilot varied and changed as the war progressed. At the start of the war it could be as little as six months (150 flying hours). On average it took between eighteen months and two years (200–320 flying hours). After receiving their commission, pilots were sent to Operational Training Units for a four- to six-week training period. American pilots flying for the RAF had issues in accepting commissions pledging 'life and loyalty to the King'. The neutrality proclamation issued by President Franklin D. Roosevelt in 1939 prevented Americans from accepting commissions, or aiding any 'belligerent nations'. The restrictions were circumvented by allowing Americans to 'pledge to obey their commander's orders'. This montage comprises an officer's commission awarded to Pilot Officer Reginald Key in July 1940 (centre), a photograph of two Battle of Britain pilots (upper right), a photograph of King George and the Queen Mother with Lord Dowding (lower right), RAF pilots of No. 222 (Natal) Squadron painting an aerial victory symbol on a panel recovered from a downed German plane (lower left) and Battle of Britain pilot Bob Doe (upper left).

PILOT'S WINGS

When an RAF pilot earned his wings, the award carried great power. The King's crown wings sewn on the uniform above the heart proved that the wearer was part of an elite club. Wearing the uniform with RAF wings was transformative. Geoffrey Wellum, a pilot of No. 92 Squadron, recalled the dizzying effect of self-admiration after his wings were sewn onto his uniform. Colin Hodgkinson, a pilot who lost both legs in an accident, credited his wings for his rehabilitation: 'Air Force Blue, at that time the most famous colour in the world … I smoothed the wings above my left breast pocket, prinked like a mannequin up and down before a glass. My God! Nothing could stop me now. I was irresistible!' William Simpson, a pilot who suffered burns during the Battle of Britain, recalled how women were attracted to 'those silver embroidered wings on the smoke-blue RAF uniform, and the little flashes of coloured ribbon beneath them … The uniform was redolent of glamour and courage. Even the breaking of our bodies was accepted as part of success rather than failure.'

The wings shown here belonged to Flying Officer John Dundas of No. 609 Squadron and are sewn to his RAF tunic dated May 1940. Dundas is credited with twelve confirmed victories, two shared destroyed, four probables and five damaged during his service. He was awarded a DFC on 9 October 1940. One month later, he shot down the German ace Helmut Wick, but was then downed by Wick's wingman, Rudi Pflanz. Both Wick and Dundas were listed as missing in action. Their remains were never found.

FLIGHT SERGEANT STRIPES

The non-commissioned rank of flight sergeant was initially devised by the Royal Flying Corps in 1912 and was carried into the RAF upon its formation in 1918. Most of the Commonwealth partner countries also adopted the flight sergeant rank. Flight sergeants flew the same aircraft types as pilot officers but were not commissioned. The issue of commissions was a point of contention between Canada and the RAF during the war. The RAF's official position was that commissions were granted 'in recognition of character, intelligence and capacity to lead, command and set a worthy example'. The RAF permitted those who washed out of pilot training to secure commissions as wireless operators, flight engineers or air gunners if they possessed such leadership capacities, but prohibited flight sergeants from receiving commissions. Canadian officials appealed against the RAF's reliance on impressionistic 'leadership qualities' and argued that 'all aircrew members should be given commissions' because 'it is not right or proper that a non-commissioned officer should be expected to perform the same duties as a commissioned officer but without the rank that goes with those responsibilities.' Roughly one-third of the pilots who flew in the Battle of Britain, and some of the battle's leading aces, were sergeant pilots. The insignia for a flight sergeant was a brass crown above the sergeant's chevrons worn on the sleeve, as depicted here. Sergeants assigned to ground crew wore only the cloth chevrons on their tunics.

AIRCRAFT
IDENTIFICATION AIDS

During the Second World War attempts were made to educate both pilots and the public in identifying aircraft and discerning friend from foe. Pilots needed to make quick judgements at high speeds about the aircraft they encountered and ground observation personnel needed to be able accurately to report enemy aircraft approaching the British coast. Flash cards, rubber aircraft models and photographic albums all helped to train pilots and ground observers rapidly to identify aircraft types.

Pilots and official spotters were not the only people trained to check the skies when they heard the sound of a plane. The public served as important 'eyes and ears' for the RAF and efforts were made to inform and educate them so aircraft could accurately be reported. Unofficial spotters learned to identify planes with decks of plane-spotter cards or the charts that were printed in newspapers and magazines, shown here. Companies produced plane-spotter premiums and aircraft spotter dials.

A FORCE OF MANY NATIONS

During the Second World War, the RAF's truly multi-national status was demonstrated by the contributions made during the Battle of Britain. As previously noted, the aircrew awarded the Battle of Britain clasp included crew from Poland, New Zealand, Canada, Czechoslovakia, Australia, Belgium, South Africa, France, Rhodesia, Jamaica and the United States. Before the end of the war, the RAF also gained pilots from Norway, Holland, Trinidad, India and thirty-three other countries. Aircrew from these countries wore easily distinguished cloth shoulder titles on their RAF uniforms that were usually black for NCOs and airmen and arched blue/grey for officers. These patches bore the name of the airman's country of origin in pale blue embroidery.

This set of Czech and Polish pilot's wings, made by the London silversmith Spink, was presented to Squadron Leader R. G. Kellett by the Polish pilot Sergeant M. B. Domagala. Kellett was a stern officer who commanded No. 303 'Polish' Squadron. As he was departing the squadron, Kellett wrote:

> We fought together through the great offensive of 1940 and I then knew that the pilots of No. 303 Squadron were not only the best but would also see me through any troubles. In the month of September, 303 Squadron was on top – no squadron from the Empire could equal the courage and skill of our pilots, no bombing could daunt our airmen.

BOMBER COMMAND

RAF Bomber Command inflicted tremendous damage on German cities, but suffered greatly for its efforts. Bomber Command experienced high casualty rates: 55,573 killed out of a total of 125,000 aircrew (a 44.4 per cent death rate), with a further 8,403 wounded in action and 9,838 becoming prisoners of war. Only 10 per cent of those serving with Bomber Command at the beginning of the war survived to 1945. Bomber Command aircrew had a worse chance of survival than a British infantry officer in the Great War. Of the Command's personnel killed during the war, 72 per cent were British, 18 per cent were Canadian, 7 per cent were Australian and 3 per cent were New Zealanders. A total of 8,305 airmen lost their lives in non-operational flying, such as training or accidents. Bomber command flew 372,650 operational sorties, and dropped almost a million tons of bombs; 8,617 of its aircraft were lost in action. The grave casualties suffered give testimony to the courage of Bomber Command's aircrews in carrying out their missions. They knew that there was little prospect of surviving a tour of thirty operations; by 1943 the odds were that just one in six were expected to survive their first tour. Only one in forty would survive a second tour. Pictured here is a 1939-dated tunic (centre) of Bomber Command's Pilot Officer Harry Graham-Hastings DFM, a logbook, 'S' brevet wing, prayer book, and photo of an aircrew wireless operator (lower left), a panoramic photo of No. 10 Squadron, and a souvenir No. 88 Squadron plaque (lower right).

MAPS

RAF pilots used many different types of map for navigation, obtained both from official and private sources. Such maps were produced on paper as well as laminated linen; special escape maps, printed on silk, were also made available that could be concealed within the lining of flight suits. The RAF used special war editions of Ordnance Survey maps produced by the army and also maps that were published for the RAF before the war. The latter had thick, brown paper covers to resist wear and were carried into the cockpit in the leg pocket of the flight suit. The example shown here, dated 1937, was part of a series produced for the RAF; it displays south-east England and London at one quarter of an inch to the mile. It belonged to Pilot Officer George Edward Hill. Hill was commissioned on 6 November 1939 and downed a German Bf 109 fighter during the Battle of France in 1940. He flew Hurricanes with No. 245 Squadron during the Battle of Britain, during which period he made use of this map. Hill was killed in action on 31 March 1944; he was just twenty-eight years old.

TYPE B FLYING HELMET

The standard flying helmet issued to RAF pilots and aircrew during the years 1936 to 1941 was the Type B, shown here. The classic design of the dark brown leather helmet with its protruding zippered ear cups became synonymous with the Battle of Britain pilots. The helmet was most often worn with the Mark IIIa goggles and the Type D oxygen mask and was equipped with a leather chinstrap and a friction-type Bennett buckle. The back of the helmet also had adjustable leather straps and buckles to tighten the fit. The Type B helmet was manufactured in four different sizes and was not factory-wired for communications equipment. Communications receivers were inserted inside the zippered earpieces that were separately applied to the helmet for a custom fit. The earpieces were insulated with chamois pads and rubber cups to reduce outside noise interference. The Type D oxygen mask was attached using the snap fasteners arrayed on each side of the helmet. Although designed for use with the Type D mask, helmets were modified at later stages in the war to allow their use with other oxygen mask variations.

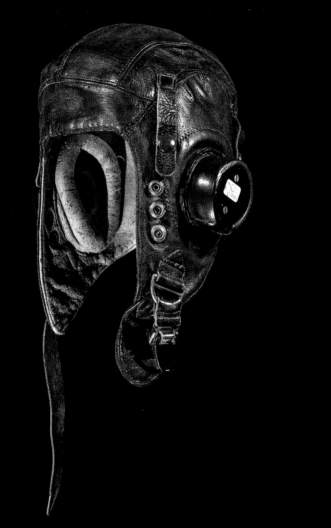

TYPE C FLYING HELMET

The Type C leather flying helmet, shown here, was issued in late 1941. Like its famous predecessor, it was made of dark brown leather and lined in smooth chamois. It marked a great improvement over the Type B both in form and function. The opening at the back of the helmet was eliminated and an elastic cord was inserted. The leather chinstrap and the Bennett buckle continued to be part of the design. Most notably, the protruding zippered earpieces were eliminated, being replaced by moulded rubber cups which allowed communications receivers to be tightly slid into position to minimise outside noise interference. The helmet was still manufactured without communications wiring and wiring apparatus (comprising heavy loom cord and plug) was needed to connect the receivers to the cockpit radio. A large, bell-shaped microphone was inserted into the oxygen mask to allow pilot voice communications. The RAF did not issue helmets with factory-wired communications systems until 1944. The Type C helmet was often worn with the Mark IV goggles and a Type E oxygen mask. The helmet had two sets of snap-fastening straps that were specially designed to accommodate the Mark IV goggles. A strap sewn to the back of the helmet held the goggles in place, reducing slippage during operations. The Type C helmet continued to be worn until the end of the war, but later RAF goggle designs rendered the forward goggle straps unnecessary.

FLYING GOGGLES

At the start of the Second World War, the standard British flight gear was outdated, having been intended mostly for use in open-cockpit aircraft. As early aircraft types were replaced by the Perspex-canopied Hurricanes and Spitfires, pilot equipment technology failed to keep pace. During the Battle of Britain, there was a lack of standardisation in the flight gear used by pilots. Both government issue items and private purchase equipment were used by pilots, dependent on supply and preference. Perhaps no items lacked uniformity as much as flying goggles. Wartime photographs document great variation in the types used during combat. Some pilots wore the basic goggles that dated back to the Great War, while others endured the Mark III version that featured a large leather face pad intended for open-cockpit flying. The goggles most often associated with the air battles of 1940 are the government-supplied Mark IIIa goggles first introduced in 1935. The Mark IIIa goggles (below) had a metal frame with leather nose support and a velveteen cushion pad; but they were often criticised by pilots because of the propensity for the celluloid lens inserts to become scratched during combat operations. The curvature of the lenses also distorted vision. Because the goggles had been designed independently of the standard flying helmet of the day, they did not fit well. RAF pilots lobbied for improvement and the Air Ministry responded with an improved design that better served the needs of the pilots, introducing the famous split-lens Mark IV goggles in June 1940. Improved variations of these split-lens goggles continued to appear up to the end of the war, culminating in the iconic Mark VIII split-lens goggles (above).

NIGHT ADAPTATION GOGGLES

In response to the German bombing raids over London, RAF fighter pilots were compelled to conduct dangerous night-time flight operations. To help acclimatise them to flying in the dark, specially made goggles were provided so that pilots awaiting missions would not have to delay operations while their eyes adjusted. The Mark Ia goggles were issued early in the war. Later, the Polaroid Corporation manufactured a rubberised goggle known as the US Type B8/M1944 goggle (above) under contract with RAF Bomber Command at a plant in London. Bomber crews usually wore the red-lens goggles (below) for about an hour before flying a mission to provide adaptation to night vision. In June 1943, Lieutenant-Colonel Edward Montgomery, a Marine Corps officer from the United States, interviewed the RAF pilots about night-fighter operations. He noted:

One thing they have developed over there that's been a tremendous help is the very heavy, very dark goggles for practicing night flying in the daytime. There are several shades of darkness to use, depending upon light conditions. On a very bright sunlit day you put these goggles on and can barely see through them at all. The British claim they have cut down their night flying accidents by ninety percent with this system. I can well imagine they did. It's much more difficult than any kind of night flying I ever saw; you just can't see anything but your instruments and the sodium lights on the runway.

FLYING SCARF

RAF pilots wore many types of flying scarf during the war. Beyond fashion, the intended purpose was the keep the pilot warm in the cockpit and to reduce neck chafing – pilots kept their necks in constant motion scanning for both enemy and friendly aircraft. During the Battle of Britain the blue-and-white polka-dot scarf (right) was very popular and can be seen in many period photographs. Pilots also wore plain white scarfs, with hand-knotted tassels, made by their sweethearts from silk parachute material (left). Wing Commander H. R. 'Dizzy' Allen recalled:

I threw off my pyjamas and dressed. This didn't take long. On top I had an RAF shirt with no collar attached. One turned the head with such frequency that a collar would have chafed the neck. Around my neck I wrapped the red silk scarf intended to alleviate the chafing, because the head was turned round so regularly to scan in the lethal area – a sector of about fifteen degrees dead astern. The rear view mirror was helpful, but only about 60 per cent effective … in this, the scarf helped. It was also part and parcel of the aura of superstition in which we lived. It had been, in fact, the seventh veil of a seven-veil dancer performing at the Empire Theatre in Chatham. She had intended to remove only six of her scarves, but I was waiting in the wings and was quicker than she … When I first put it round my neck it stank of cheap perfume and perspiration and nearly gave me anoxia, but on the first sortie while wearing it I shot down two Messerschmitts or thought I had. So it became my talisman.

RAF SHIRT

The standard RAF officer's shirt was of a light blue/grey weave, with double-cuff long sleeves and a detachable collar affixed by metal studs. Other than a shift from white to blue, the design of the RAF shirt remained unchanged from the 1920s. The long tails found on the shirt were intended to allow additional material for repair or the manufacture of a replacement collar. There were several private tailors, such as T. M. Lewin, Gieves & Hawkes and other Saville Row tailors in London, that made high-quality officer's shirts. Some RAF officers are known to have had their collars stitched on for comfort but this was against RAF regulations. Many pilots also left the front button of their shirt undone while on combat operations, as the stiffly starched shirt collars had a tendency to shrink when wet. The equipment worn by a pilot who might need to bail out over the Channel made survival challenging enough without risking asphyxiation by shirt collar. The private-purchase shirt pictured here belonged to the aforementioned Battle of Britain ace John Dundas, who flew with No. 609 Squadron.

RAF SWEATER

Officially known as the 'Frock, White Aircrew 22G/63', the RAF sweater became one of the most familiar and heroically romantic items to become associated with Battle of Britain pilots. The off-white aircrew sweater was worn under the service dress tunic or flying suit for an extra layer of warmth, and was worn from 1940 to 1945. The American Eagle Squadron pilot Wilson 'Bill' Edwards, recalled: 'I flew in my uniform almost all the time. I usually had my 'Irving Jacket,' which was a heavy lined jacket to keep warm and I often wore a pullover turtleneck sweater, especially in the winter, since the Spitfire and the Hurricane had no cockpit heaters.' The frock comprised two separate front and back pieces that were coarsely sewn together. The neck piece was sewn on in a straight line across the shoulders rather than following a more natural curved line along the neck. The seams were canvas reinforced where the neck joined the body of the frock. The result was a tight-fitting sweater made from stiff wool, with arm pieces made from a single piece of fabric that was sewn on the inside. The cuffs were knitted rather than sewn on separately. Despite being officially replaced by a navy blue version in March 1944, the white knitted frock continued to be worn by pilots of all RAF commands in every theatre of the war.

SHAVING KIT

Even during active flight operations, RAF aircrew were expected to maintain a clean-cut appearance in conformance with Air Ministry rules. Regulations required a clean chin, but pilots were permitted a moustache as long as it did not interfere with use of the oxygen mask. The 1940 edition of the King's Regulations and Air Council Instructions required that 'the hair on the head will be kept well cut and trimmed. Beard or whiskers will not be worn. If a moustache is worn the upper lip will be entirely unshaven.' In his memoirs, the RAF fighter ace Robert Stanford-Tuck wrote: 'Only a moustache was allowed after permission was granted. The moustache had to be of the handlebar model.' Safety razors had been available even before the Great War and officers often brought private-purchase shaving kits into service that were presentation gifts from loved ones. The fine kit shown here, in brown leather, features several silver-plated capped-glass vials for powder and lotions, along with a razor case, all fitted into separate sleeves for organisation and care during transit. The officer stamped a black-inked RAF wing on the inside cloth-covered flap of the holdall. The steel shaving mirror was presented in a leather sleeve embossed with the gold insignia of the Royal Canadian Air Force.

DITCH WHISTLE

RAF combat aircrew were issued whistles manufactured by J. Hudson & Company of Birmingham. The company's main plant took a direct hit from a German bomb on the evening of 27 October 1940 and suffered major damage. The whistles were marked with the Air Ministry crown and various RAF stock numbers and were popularly known as 'Acme' whistles – taken from the Greek word meaning 'high point'. The whistles were important survival items intended for use by airmen compelled to bail out of their aircraft. A downed pilot might blow the whistle when in the water to attract rescue ships, or on land to help gather other aircrew together. Originally, they were intended to be attached to the life jacket, but aircrew soon attached them to the hook on the collar of the battledress jacket. The early types were the long-tube type as used by British police, but these were found to stick to the lips in cold water and were replaced by the type pictured here or plastic versions made to the same design. This example belonged to Pilot Officer P. J. Simpson who flew with No. 111 and No. 64 Squadrons during the Battle of Britain. Simpson claimed four enemy aircraft during the battle and shared in the destruction of another six. He was shot down during the battle and survived a forced landing of his Hurricane on Woodcote Golf Course near Epsom, Surrey, on 18 August 1940.

1930 PATTERN
FLYING SUIT

The 1930 Pattern Flying Suit, known as the 'Sidcot Suit', was made of lightweight green cotton that was waterproofed and lined with linen. The 1930 Pattern was modelled on the earlier flight suit of the Great War and was of a one piece overall construction with a diagonal zip front, sleeves and legs. It featured a large flap collar to which a detachable fleece collar could be buttoned. The suit had large map pockets on the left breast and on the thigh (which also doubled as handwarmer pockets). The suit was either worn over the service dress uniform or in association with two button-in linings. The bold design of one of these linings earned it the sobriquet 'Teddy Bear Suit', because of its oversized rumpled design made of synthetic fur. These were popular with Bomber Command crews and were worn with the fur on the inside to retain maximum body heat during high-altitude flying.

The example of the 1930 Pattern Flying Suit shown here is dated 1940 and is typical of those worn by the Battle of Britain pilots. During the early stages of the war, some squadrons had their squadron badges sewn to the left breast of the suit. A fine example of such a suit, belonging to Wing Commander Gordon L. Sinclair, is in the collection of the Imperial War Museum, London.

IRVIN PARACHUTE

There were two different types of parachute that were most extensively used during the Second World War: the chest and seat-pack types. Seat-pack parachutes were used primarily by pilots. The harness for both types of parachute was a double thickness white cotton/linen webbing with metal attachment fittings. A quick release box (QRB) was positioned over the abdomen, and two web straps passed over the shoulders and two more around the upper legs, with all the straps coming together at the QRB. The Type C seat-pack parachute was considered an innovative design because it enabled the wearer to discard the entire pack quickly with a simple turn and punch of the buckle. This was important in the event of an emergency landing in high winds or water. The parachute type most often used by RAF fighter pilots during the war was the Type C-2. This model was an improvement over the earlier design and featured a D-ring pull that was located at the waist rather than the more difficult-to-reach position at the lower hip. The seat pack was dual purpose in that it also served as a seat cushion in the fighter aircraft, thereby adding to pilot comfort. Parachutes were manufactured by Irving Air Chute of Great Britain Limited and Gerald Quilter (G.Q.) Parachute Company. The silk parachute shown here was made by Irving (note that when the Irvin company registered in 1919, the letter 'g' was erroneously added to the company's name) and is Air Ministry marked and dated 27 January 1938. All aircrew canopies were constructed of white silk until 1943, when nylon gradually replaced the early war issue.

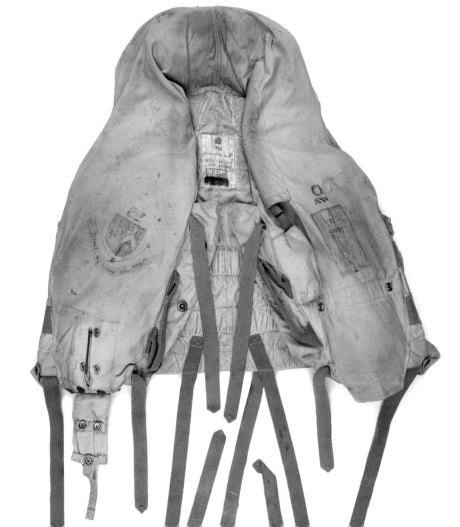

1941 PATTERN 'MAE WEST' LIFE JACKET

During the Battle of Britain, RAF pilots wore the old 1932 Pattern life jacket. It was a clumsy, green cotton quill waistcoat that closed with three buttons and two buckled straps and featured a flotation bladder that needed to be inflated orally by the user. As a result of the limitations, pilots awaiting scramble usually inflated the bladders partially before buckling into the cockpit. The resulting bulging appearance of the vest earned the nickname 'Mae West' in honour of the buxom actress. In July 1941, the Life Jacket Mark I was introduced and remained the primary RAF life jacket for the rest of the war. Life jackets were treated as part of an airman's kit and they were often decorated with squadron insignia, cartoons or the owner's name. The example shown here (from the Australian War Memorial collections) belonged to Royal Australian Air Force (RAAF) Flight Lieutenant T. E. W. Howes of No. 70 Squadron, RAF and features his name, an inked drawing of an observer brevet wing, a Distinguished Flying Cross (DFC) ribbon and a drawing of a shield in red and blue. A red ribbon scroll written in black ink under the shield reads: 'What We Have We Hold'.

OXYGEN MASK

Few pieces of equipment used by RAF airmen were as essential as the oxygen mask. A number of different types were used during the war, ranging from the green fabric Type D, which was used extensively during the Battle of Britain, to this Type E, which was adopted in February 1942 and made of grey/green rubber. The Type E mask was the first RAF oxygen mask to use a demand-based flow system, whereby oxygen was released from the supply tank only when the wearer inhaled. The mask was prone to freezing due to design faults related to the shared inlet/outlet tube and was the subject of more design modifications than any other piece of RAF personal equipment. A Type G mask was issued by the RAF in the spring of 1943 that featured many improvements. This mask remained in service until well after the war. Wing Commander Terence Cane of No. 234 Squadron recalled how he attempted to bale out of his crippled Spitfire over the Channel in 1940, only to discover that he couldn't release his oxygen mask, and had to climb back into the aircraft to free himself: 'I couldn't find the parachute ripcord. Panic set in, I was falling through cloud … if I'd been three seconds later pulling the ripcord, I wouldn't be here.' Kane was rescued and captured by the Germans, spending the remainder of the war as a POW.

1933 PATTERN FLYING GAUNTLETS

Pilots wore gloves or long flying gauntlets to protect their hands during flight operations. During the Battle of Britain, they often complained about the gloves provided to them by the Air Ministry because they did not fit well over the sleeves of the heavy insulated shearling Irvin jackets. As a result, pilots often decided to fly without the gloves and sometimes suffered serious burns to their hands in cockpit fires. The standard type of glove worn during the Battle of Britain was the 1933 Pattern flying gauntlet, but many pilots abandoned the gloves in favour of the chamois linings that were issued with the gloves, wearing them to retain better feel over their aircraft. The 1941 Pattern flying gauntlet was a marked design improvement, and proved that the Air Ministry was listening to pilot feedback about equipment. The new gauntlet (shown here) was similar to the earlier model but was elasticated at the wrist and featured a long diagonal zipper so that the Irvin jacket could be tucked into the glove. Some pilots still resisted wearing them, fearing that the heavy leather prevented physical contact with the aircraft controls, but the new design proved so popular with the fresh pilots flooding the ranks of the RAF that manufacturers had difficulty keeping up with demand. The gloves were so prized and prone to theft by workers that left-hand and right-hand gloves were produced at separate factories; this explains why many surviving pairs of the gauntlets are mismatched in colour. A Bomber Command pilot who completed flight training in 1941 recalled that upon his commission he received 'three pairs of gloves (silk inner, then wool, then the leather gauntlets on top)'.

TYPE P8 AIRCRAFT COMPASS

The type P8 compass, shown here, was standard equipment in the Fighter Command aircraft of the RAF. Both Spitfires and Hurricanes used these Mark II compasses to navigate during combat operations and to find their way home. The tubes inside the compass were filled with radium powder and provided luminescence during night operations. A brass Air Ministry label was affixed to the rim. The compass was designed for use anywhere in the world, and could take into account the angle of dip induced by the poles. Carrying boxes were made of wood, and were specially designed to protect this essential navigation device. The RAF map dated 1942 used as a backdrop was used in a bombing run over Munich, Germany.

Various compass types were manufactured for the Air Ministry; the 'P' series were pilots' compasses, while the 'O' series were intended for observers. During the war, compasses were produced by several different makers. Those used by the RAF were aperiodic compasses, which settled on a true course following a turn without the need for manual overcompensation.

OFFICER'S PEAKED CAP

RAF officers wore this peaked cap made of blue-grey fabric with a black mohair band. The peak was fabric-covered for officers (as here) and black leather for other ranks, such as warrant officers. The early officer's cap had a green cardboard stiffener to support the fabric visor. The officer's cap badge featured a brass eagle surrounded by laurel leaves and topped with a crown. Non-commissioned officers substituted the RAF monogram for the eagle. Warrant officers had a simple gilt metal version of the officer's cap badge.

The peaked cap became a symbol of the RAF pilot's service and a worn and battered appearance was considered evidence of experience. Many pilots accelerated the ageing process and removed the wire frame from inside the cap to give a 'crushed' appearance. Caps were usually worn at a jaunty angle, in subtle opposition to rigid RAF regulations.

This cap belonged to Battle of Britain ace Johnny Kent, a Canadian who joined the RAF in 1935. He was awarded the Air Force Cross (AFC) – even before the war started – for his work in developing barrage balloons; he assisted the nascent technology by deliberately piloting his aircraft into collisions with the balloons on 300 occasions. Kent served with No. 303 'Polish' Squadron and later commanded No. 92 Squadron and had thirteen confirmed victories with three probables and three damaged during the war.

FORAGE CAPS

RAF flying officers, NCOs and enlisted personnel all wore cloth service caps of a similar design. The RAF officer's forage cap was made of barathea wool and featured a two-piece badge design of the King's crown over an RAF eagle (above). The other ranks' forage cap was cut of rough blue/grey serge with a stamped brass RAF cap badge affixed (below). Commonwealth countries applied their own distinctive badges to these caps and as an economy measure during the war, these badges were also manufactured in black plastic, being worn both on the forage cap and the beret that was used during the war's final years. Both versions of the caps featured two RAF buttons on the facing. The officer's cap shown here belonged to Flying Officer John Dundas. Both forage caps are dated 1940 and are typical of those worn during the Battle of Britain.

"Be strong and of a good courage, for the
Lord thy God is with thee whither-
soever thou goest."

S/L A. Montague-Bull

R.A.F.

ON ACTIVE SERVICE

Issued by
THE NATIONAL BIBLE SOCIETY
OF SCOTLAND

A Royal Message
from
H.M. King George VI.
about
The Bible—The Book of Books

"To all serving in my forces by sea,
or land, or in the air, and indeed
to all my people engaged
defence of the Realm
the reading of
centuries th
wholesom
fluen

NEW TESTAMENT

TESTAMENT

Small Bibles, or Active Service Testaments, were provided to RAF aircrew throughout the war. The small-format books were intended to be carried in a uniform pocket or stored with an airman's kit, and provided comfort during difficult times away from home and family. The New Testament shown here was published by The National Bible Society of Scotland and contains a 'Royal Message from King George VI'. It belonged to Arthur Montagu-Smith, an RAF pilot who flew Boulton Paul Defiants during the Battle of Britain and conducted the first Wellington attack on a German submarine of the war in October 1939. He joined the RAF in 1935 and served as squadron adjutant for No. 99 Squadron. Montagu-Smith commanded No. 264 Squadron during the Battle of Britain. His brother Alan served in the army and was killed at Dunkirk. When Arthur died in January 2014, *The Times* noted: 'Like most of his generation, the war was a defining element of his life and the Royal Air Force remained a constant thread, a fact eloquently illustrated when, while whizzing along an empty country road under a moonlit sky, he insisted on switching off the vehicle's headlight to demonstrate the exhilarating art of flying by the light of a bomber's moon.'

1936 PATTERN FLYING BOOTS

The 1936 Pattern flying boots are the footwear most often associated with RAF pilots during the Battle of Britain. The black leather, fleece-lined boots were pull-on style, with leather pull-tabs sewn inside the boot and a tightening strap to ensure a good fit. At the beginning of the war many pilots wore their service dress shoes during flight operations, but those that could afford (or who could otherwise acquire) a pair of 1936 Pattern boots were the fortunate of 'The Few'. This pair belonged to the RAF ace Johnny Kent and were privately purchased. The boots are of much higher quality than those manufactured for and provided by the Air Ministry.

1940 PATTERN FLYING BOOTS

The 1940 Pattern flying boot was simply constructed from brown suede and was heavily lined in fleece and was an improvement over previous designs. The foot section was completely encased in a rubber coating that was intended both to help insulate the boot and to prevent aircrew from slipping as they performed their duties during flight. The full-length zip allowed pilots to tuck their trousers or Irvin trousers into the boots for warmth during high-altitude operations. While practical, the boots lacked the dashing appeal of the full leather 1936 Pattern and were more popular with aircrew than fighter pilots. Most notably, the loose fit of the boot, while providing comfort, contributed to the propensity for the boots to slip off during parachute descent. As a result, a new design of the boot adopted in 1941 featured leather ankle straps (which were retroactively applied to existing stock of the old model) to address the problem and ensure a tighter fit. The 1941 modification added to the poor style of the boots and the leather straps that were added sometimes became entangled in aircraft equipment and wiring.

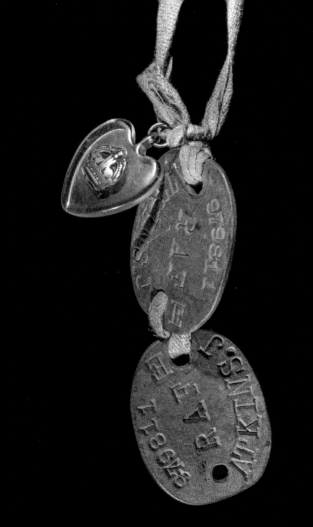

GOOD LUCK CHARMS

An airman's dog tags, a heart pendant made from an aircraft's Perspex windscreen and a brass crown made from a cap badge and carried for good luck and are pictured here. Fighter pilots could be superstitious and many carried good luck charms and talisman mascots with them in the cockpit. Geoffrey Wellum would perch his Eeyore – a stuffed animal modelled on a character from *Winnie the Pooh* – on his map case during flights. Wellum recalled that he always had confidence when accompanied by the mascot. Pictured below is a stuffed bear nicknamed 'Bea' that was carried by Flight Lieutenant Stephen Beaumont of No. 609 Squadron during the Battle of Britain. When he donated the bear to a charity auction in 1996, Beaumont noted that it had flown on many combat sorties.

A DOG NAMED BILL

A PILOT'S BEST FRIEND

During the war, many RAF aircrew adopted pets as good luck charms, squadron mascots and companions. Wing Commander Guy Gibson of No. 617 Squadron felt great affection for the squadron's mascot, a black Labrador that sometimes accompanied him on training missions. The dog enjoyed the taste of beer and had its own bowl in the officers' mess. The montage opposite features (at centre) a 1943 cartoon book entitled *A Dog Named Bill* that illustrates the story of an RAF squadron dog. The book is framed by other images of wartime mascots showing (clockwise, from top right) a colour photograph of the Canadian ace Johnnie Johnson with his black Labrador Sally; a Polish sergeant pilot with his dog; Flying Sergeant George 'Grumpy' Unwin with his Alsatian, Flash; a panoramic photograph of an RCAF squadron with their mascot, dated 14 September 1940; the smiling Pilot Officer Roger Boulding with his cocker spaniel companion Sam; in the sepia snapshot, the RAF ace Denys 'Kill 'em' Gillam holding his dog; and finally a movie studio photograph of Scuffy, who belonged to a member of RAF aircrew who was killed in action. Scuffy had appeared in a British film produced before the war. While dogs proved the most popular companions, RAF pilots adopted a veritable zoo of mascots consisting of goats, lambs, monkeys, kangaroos, lion cubs and lizards during the war. Squadron dogs were so important to morale that they are remembered in a statue at the Battle of Britain Memorial at Capel-le-Ferne, Kent.

COMMONWEALTH AIR UNITS

Before the Battle of Britain, the British Commonwealth Air Training Plan (BCATP) was created to train pilots and aircrew in areas immune from enemy attack. The programme trained nearly half of the pilots, navigators and aircrew who served with the various British flying forces during the Second World War.

The Royal New Zealand Air Force (RNZAF) contributed nearly three thousand pilots to the RAF, while a further 1,500 pilots trained under the programme were retained for service in New Zealand. More than 7,900 New Zealanders were sent to Canada for training and served as pilots and aircrew – about 5 per cent of the 131,000 aircrew who trained in Canada under the BCATP.

The BCATP nations retained their international identities in wings and cap insignia. This photograph shows an RAF uniform dated 1943 with RNZAF wings, with a DFM and 1939–45 Star ribbon bar over a brass Pathfinder badge. The Pathfinders were elite squadrons of bombers that guided the RAF formations to their targets. A 1943 RCAF forage cap and scarf from No. 8 Service Flying Training School in Canada are also shown.

The success of the BCATP programme can be understood when considering the RAF's No. 602 'City of Glasgow' Squadron. It began the war comprising almost entirely Scottish and English pilots, but by late 1942 there was only a single Scot serving in a unit of Canadians, New Zealanders, Australians, South Africans, French, Caribbeans, Czechs, Poles, Irish and Norwegians.

RAF ESCAPE AND
EVASION AIDS

A pilot who successfully bailed out or survived a crash landing in enemy-controlled territory needed to keep calm and move quickly to evade hostile patrols. The RAF provided aircrew with a number of escape and evasion tools including a small compass concealed inside a uniform button, trouser-fly buttons that were magnetised to serve as a makeshift compass, silk maps that could be hidden inside uniform linings, and specially designed escape boots (shown here). Designed by Major Clayton Hutton at MI9, they first appeared in 1942 and were a full-length flying boot with a small pocket knife included inside the right boot. This knife was used to cut away the top-most portion of the boot to separate the suede leggings from the black leather shoe section; the evading pilot might thus appear to be wearing civilian shoes. One of the problems with the new boot was that the high quality of the black shoes stood in stark contrast to the footwear of struggling Europeans whose lives and economies had been devastated by war. The fleece linings inside the shoes also made walking long distances very difficult. The 1943 Pattern escape boots continued to be worn by RAF pilots well into the postwar period.

The items shown here include a battered late-war example of the compass that fitted into the back of the RAF tunic button; a magnetised fly button from the battledress trousers used to determine general course and direction when suspended from a string; and a folded silk escape map dated 1943. These maps were either worn as scarves or were sewn into the lining of aircrew uniforms and flight suits. Several bloodstains are visible on this example.

SCRAMBLE BELL

During the summer of 1940, a common sound at RAF fighter airfields in Britain was the ringing of the station bell. This was usually positioned near the dispersal huts and was rung as a warning of incoming German raids. When the bell rang, signalling the order to 'scramble', the young RAF pilots would run in full kit to their waiting aircraft, strap themselves into the cockpit with the assistance of the ground crew and then rumble down the grass runway to gain altitude as quickly as possible. Many of these bells were painted red; traces are clearly visible on this example, which is marked with the Air Ministry crown and is dated 1940. It appears that the bells were dated for the year of production from 1936 to 1945. Many bear the manufacturer's mark of 'A.T.W.' Surviving film footage taken during the Battle of Britain documents a scramble bell being rung with the chalked inscription: 'Don't Come and Tell, Ring This Like Hell!'

This original example belonged to a former American fighter pilot, Lieutenant-Colonel Michael F. Moffitt, who commanded a United States Air Force (USAF) detachment at RAF Lindholme, Doncaster, in 1956. The bell was found in storage and was remounted for use on the flightline to warn of fires and other emergencies. Moffitt was presented with the bell upon his departure from Lindholme. During the Battle of Britain, RAF Lindholme had served as the home airfield of No. 50 Squadron, and later No. 408 Squadron (RCAF).

GUINEA PIG CLUB

The Guinea Pig Club was founded in 1941. All club members were RAF or Commonwealth aircrew who had gone through experimental reconstructive plastic surgery at the Queen Victoria Hospital in East Grinstead. The men were treated by the pioneering surgeon Archibald McIndoe. Plastic surgery had been used during the Great War, but McIndoe took the techniques of reconstruction to an entirely different level. He achieved great respect for his work in treating aircrew that had been severely burned by gas-fuelled cockpit fires or disfigured by crashes. McIndoe was revered by his patients. Established initially as a drinking association – because McIndoe allowed beer in the hospital – the Guinea Pig Club pulled together airmen that had suffered traumatic injuries to support each other as they recovered or endured painful procedures. The 'guinea pig' aspect referred to the experimental nature of the surgical methods. Membership was open to all Allied aircrew who had suffered burns or facial disfigurement. McIndoe served as president, while it was stipulated that the secretary should be a patient with burned fingers in order to minimise note taking, and the treasurer should be a member without legs so that they could not abscond with club funds. Pictured top left is the cigarette case Sergeant Pilot Bob Beardsley of No. 610 Squadron presented to his wife at Christmas 1940. Beardsley crash-landed twice during the Battle of Britain. Also shown is a photograph of Dr McIndoe (centre right, with glasses) celebrating with Guinea Pig Club pilots and a commemorative Guinea Pig reunion plate (top right).

SURVIVOR CLUBS

In addition to the Guinea Pig Club there were three other unofficial clubs that flourished during the war. These organisations were open to those that could satisfy membership criteria based on their success in escaping from disabled aircraft and on surviving a variety of traumatic situations that might confront airmen in the course of flight operations.

The Caterpillar Club celebrated the survival of those who used parachutes. It was named in honour of the silkworm that provided the material for latter. Irving Air Chute of Great Britain Limited and other parachute manufacturers participated in the club and provided pins, certificates and membership cards to those who applied to join. Each member of the club was presented with a card signed by the company founder Leslie Irvin and a gold caterpillar pin with red amethyst eyes (centre right). By the end of the war, more than 34,000 Irvin pins had been presented to Allied airmen. The Switlik Parachute Company also issued caterpillar pins but only twenty-five of these were awarded to RAF aircrew.

The Goldfish Club was formed in 1942 and provided a cloth badge (centre) to aircrew who had been rescued from the sea. A row of blue cord was added for each subsequent sea rescue. Regulations prevented wearing the badge on uniforms so crews often wore it under the flap of their uniform pocket.

The Late Arrivals Club was formed in 1941 to celebrate airmen who had evaded capture. A locally crafted, silver winged boot insignia (top left) was presented and worn on the left breast of the flying suit.

THE WAAF AT WAR

Members of the Women's Auxiliary Air Force (known as WAAFs), which was formed in June 1939, initially performed duties as clerks, orderlies and drivers, but their role expanded as the war required additional men to serve on the frontlines. WAAFs operated telegraph and wireless devices, and intercepted codes and ciphers. They served as ground crew, weather analysts and worked in the radar control system as reporters and plotters. The work of the WAAFs was essential to the RAF's success during the war. In December 1941 the National Service Act provided for the conscription of women between the ages of twenty and thirty to support the war effort. Women could either engage in factory war work, or join the WAAF or its army or naval equivalents. WAAFs were paid two-thirds of the pay of their male counterparts in the RAF. At peak strength in 1943, WAAF numbers exceeded 180,000, with two thousand women enlisting each week. Nearly 220,000 women had served in the WAAF by the end of 1945, with an estimated 700 who died from various causes during active service. Pictured here is a WAAF uniform tunic dated 1942 and a portrait photograph of its owner, a WAAF identified only as 'M. Payne'. The tunic has RAF shoulder eagle insignia, Leading Aircraftwoman (LACW) rank insignia on each sleeve, and a wireless operator trade patch on its right sleeve.

TO A DAUGHTER NEVER SEEN

If I should never see you in this world,
If war's inconsequence should claim me, too
God grant me this, that I may come to you
When you're asleep, with tiny fingers curled
Around your pillow, with the moon's white rays
Making a halo round your golden hair.
Give me an hour to let me watch you there
Midway between this life and death's dark ways.

And then, perhaps, when many years have passed
You will recall a long forgotten dream,
Of how a stranger came when you were fast
Asleep, and stooped and kissed your curly head
And as you think of me there'll be a gleam
Of light upon the valley of the dead.

DIARY

The King's Regulations prohibited military personnel from maintaining journals or diaries, fearing that they could provide valuable intelligence information to the enemy if captured. Despite such restrictions, stationers produced pocket diaries and journals specially designed to be used by pilots and airmen during the war. During the Battle of Britain, the pace of operations was such that it was nearly impossible for a pilot or airman to maintain a personal journal. The Battle of Britain pilots George Barclay and Denis Wissler are known to have kept diaries during the battle, but most pilots were unable to balance flight operations with diary composition. Even letters sent by pilots during the Battle of Britain period are very scarce.

This journal belonged to Flying Officer W. G. Harrison and begins with a poem that he wrote for his daughter in case he should not return. Harrison was a medical officer assigned to an RAF Air Search and Rescue (ASR) squadron. He survived the war.

AIR MAIL

EXAMINER 6406

R.C.A.F. OVERSEAS.
August 30th.

Aug 30

My Dearest,
Letter No 18. Still red still night - actually still letter no 17 as I have just folded it up and stuck down the labels. ... its all about today the daily roster. ...

SECURITY THINK- BEFORE YOU WRITE !!

BY AIR MAIL
AIR LETTER
IF ANYTHING IS ENCLOSED THIS LETTER WILL BE SENT BY ORDINARY MAIL

R.A.F. CENSOR. 463

MRS. BOWDERY
123 MATHESON AVE
WINNIPEG
MANITOBA
CANADA

I hope you realize how you are keeping me from my trundle bed - if you do it doesn't matter 'cause I like writing to you ... have I told you that before ...

ARMED FORCES
AIR LETTER
AIR MAIL

LETTERS

RAF pilots and airmen had little free time during combat operations, but some took advantage of the time they did have to write letters to loved ones. Pete Brothers, a flight commander who shot down eight German aircraft remembered: 'You didn't have time to sit down and write out what was happening. If you weren't airborne, then you were in the bar or trying to catch some sleep. We were just ordinary chaps doing what we had to do.' Pilots and airmen enjoyed receiving letters and hearing news from home; this was very important for maintaining morale and the RAF encouraged correspondence. Because of concerns about letters falling into enemy hands and providing sensitive military details, those sent home by pilots and airmen were censored, and serving crews were cautioned about the nature of what they should include in their letters. Officers were able to self-censor their letters 'on their honour', but those of lower rank had their letters reviewed and censored by officers who became intimately familiar with the personal affairs of their men. Letters were usually written in pencil or fountain pen either on plain paper or on stationery embossed with the RAF insignia or squadron identification. The letters sent home were treasured by families and were often numbered in order of receipt. Some surviving collections of correspondence comprise hundreds of letters sent over the course of the war. The letters in the collection pictured here were sent home during 1944–5 by Flight Lieutenant Roger Bowdrey who served with No. 200 Squadron in India, Burma and Ceylon.

Air Publication 1548
March, 1938
2nd edition *June, 1941*

NOT TO BE CARRIED IN
AIRCRAFT

INSTRUCTIONS and **GUIDE** to **ALL OFFICERS** and **AIRMEN**
of **THE ROYAL AIR FORCE** regarding **PRECAUTIONS** to be
taken in the event of falling into the hands of an **ENEMY**

Issued for the information and guidance of all concerned.

the Air Council

tion is to be issued
duties might take
ade to every officer
during the period
has a copy.
ll other personnel have a bound
down herein.

Dear Mr. Arnold,

I know that you will be passing through a period of acute anxiety since you have heard that your son has been reported missing. It may mean waiting a fair time before you hear any further news. I do assure you that you are in our thoughts and prayers, and I believe it is your duty to hold on to the hope that he is safe and sound until more certain information can be given you. So often good news has been received after men have been missing for a very long time and I hope with you that you will have a re-assuring message very soon.

I am,

Yours sincerely,

E. W. Platt,

Station Chaplain.

MISSING-IN-ACTION LETTERS

There were letters that families did not want to receive. An officer appearing unexpectedly at the door would be a heart-stopping experience, while a telegram or official letter would be torn open with dread. Sometimes the communication was routine, but as the war progressed, more and more letters and telegrams were sent informing families that a loved one had been killed in action. In other cases, a letter might give the details of a reported loss and note only that the airman was 'missing believed killed'. Such letters were usually sent by the airman's squadron commander. While a family might hold out hope that their relative was safe, the uncertainty lingered; many never learned the definitive details of what had happened to their loved one. The letter shown here, from RAF Wyton's Station Chaplain E. W. Platt, relates to the reported loss of Sergeant Tony Arnold of No. 40 Squadron, and is addressed to his father. Arnold went missing on 29 August 1941 when his Wellington bomber crashed near Mulheim, Germany. The pilot and two crew members were killed, but Arnold and two others survived and were taken prisoner and interred at Stalag VIIIB. He was released in 1945. Shown here is a photograph of Sergeant Arnold (lower left), his warrant officer patch (upper left), an Air Ministry guide for downed aircrew and German POW identification tag (upper right) and Arnold's air gunner brevet wing (lower right).

IRVIN JACKET

RAF pilots wore a variety of clothing in the cockpit that was intended to keep them comfortable during cold, high-altitude flights. Flying suits of all types were worn, as well as the two-piece Irvin suit (introduced in 1938), comprising a jacket and trousers made of thick-pile fleece coated with a brown waterproof dye. The suit was produced by many companies but was named after the famous parachute manufacturer after it was awarded an early production contract. The suit was very popular with Bomber Command airmen, but Fighter Command pilots preferred wearing just the jacket over the top of their flight suit overalls or service uniforms.

A new suit design was produced during the war with extra seams on the sleeves. This allowed the factories producing the jackets to reduce costs by permitting smaller cuts of material to be used. Although the jacket was officially available only to bomber crews after late 1943, the Irvin continued to be worn and is another of the iconic items associated with the RAF.

This Irvin jacket belonged to Squadron Leader Vaclav Slouf, a Czech pilot who flew with the French Air Force during the Battle of France in 1940. Slouf scored four victories over France and made his way to Britain by boat after France fell. He joined No. 312 Squadron and participated in the Battle of Britain. He was promoted to command the squadron in November 1944 before returning to Czechoslovakia in 1945. He was forced to flee when the Communists took over in 1948 and returned to Britain, retiring from the RAF in 1958.

PILOT'S FLYING
LOG BOOK

Form 447 B.

NAME *Reid A. J.*

RANK & No. F/O 186133

ROYAL AIR FORCE

FLYING CLOTHING CARD

Date of Issue
and
Unit Stamp

ACCOUNTANT OFFICER
31 OCT 1941
ROYAL AIR FORCE TORQUAY

Signature of Accountant Officer   F/O

R.A.F. FORM 2520C
OFFICER

ROYAL AIR FORCE
SERVICE AND RELEASE BOOK

Rank F/O.

Personal Number 186133.

Surname REID

Initials A. G.

Class of Release "A"

Age and Service Group No. 23.

PILOT'S FLYING LOG BOOK

The Pilot's Flying Log Book documented a pilot's career from his initial training flights through combat operations to discharge. Every aspect of his training was logged therein and certified by his instructor or commanding officer, and it detailed his experiences and accomplishments. RAF pilots logged hours flown and in which type of aircraft, and all of the columns were totalled in a neat and meticulous hand. When a book had been filled, a second book would be added to the pilot's kit; long-serving officers accumulated a library of logbooks that chronicled every hour of their flight experience. During the war, the flight logs of pilots and aircrew missing in action were sent to a central RAF depository. Sadly, if not claimed by family members, they were destroyed in the postwar period. While the formality of the books left little room for creative expression, a Bomber Command crewman once documented a particularly difficult mission that involved severed fuel lines and the serious damage inflicted by German flak by writing at the end of one entry, 'There is no future in this.'

The logbook illustrated here, along with the King's crown wing (centre right), squadron photograph, (top left) flying clothing card (lower left) and service and release book (lower right), all belonged to Flying Officer A. G. Reid (pictured top right), a Scot who served with the RAF from 1940 to 1945 and flew Hurricane fighters.

Sgt Franszisek J. (Polish).

SECRET.   FORM F

COMBAT REPORT.

Sector Serial No.	(A)	N/A
Serial No. of Order detailing Flight or Squadron to Patrol	(B)	N/A
Date	(C)	2.9.40
Flight, Squadron	(D) Flight :B	Sqdn. : 303
Number of Enemy Aircraft	(E)	9
Type of Enemy Aircraft	(F)	Me 109
Time Attack was delivered	(G)	1750
Place Attack was delivered	(H)	Dover – Channel
Height of Enemy	(J)	12000
Enemy Casualties	(K)	1 Me 109 destroyed
Our Casualties Aircraft	(L)	Nil
Personnel	(M)	Nil
GENERAL REPORT	(R)	

GENERAL REPORT.

I was green two. I was rearguard in search formation. Above Dover
I saw two Me 109's in front of me at the same height. I attacked
one head on firing short bursts at 500 yds closing to 100.
He broke away down left. I followed hitting his port fuselage.
He continued diving and turned towards France. I closed and attacked
again. A great cloud of black smoke rose from his engine and he went
down into the sea two or three kilometers from the shore. No pilot
was seen to leave the E/A.

                                   2 SEP 1940

                              Signature   Franszisek

                         O.C.   { Section Franszisek Sgt
                                 { Flight green
                                 { Squadron 303   Squadron No.

(3447—1611) Wt. 27685—2533 560 Pads 5/39 T.S. 706   FORM 1151

COMBAT REPORTS

During the Battle of Britain, pilots were interviewed by RAF intelligence officers or the station adjutant after every combat mission, and a report was filled out and signed. The information gleaned from these documents was used to examine enemy aerial combat techniques as well as to record RAF aerial victories and losses. The pilots signed and attested to the accuracy of the reports, which were classified as 'Secret.' On the combat report pictured here, the RAF clerk has mistyped the Czech pilot's name. The report, dated 2 September 1940, is signed by Flying Sergeant Josef Frantisek who flew with No. 303 'Polish' RAF Squadron. Frantisek, an accomplished and highly regarded pilot, had served in the Czech Air Force in the 1930s and joined the Polish Air Force in 1939. He was killed on 8 October 1940 – reportedly while trying to perform an aerial stunt to impress his girlfriend. At the time of his death, Frantisek was the highest-scoring ace of the Battle of Britain, having achieved seventeen victories in just twenty-seven days.

ACE OF BATTLE

During the Second World War, a fighter pilot who scored five or more aerial victories was designated an 'ace'. In the Battle of Britain, 188 RAF fighter pilots earned that distinction – 8 per cent of those who flew. About 2,300 enemy aircraft were shot down during the battle and about 39 per cent of the 2,332 RAF pilots who flew fighter aircraft had success in downing at least one enemy plane. The number of pilots who scored more than a single victory, however, comprised less than 15 per cent of those engaged. A total of 237 RAF pilots who fought in the battle attained 'ace' status later in the war. Three RAF pilots became 'aces in a day' by shooting down five enemy aircraft in 24 hours. Pilot Officer William Dudley Williams joined the RAFVR as an 'Airman under Pilot Training' in April 1938 and was called to full-time service at the outbreak of war. He joined No. 152 Squadron at Acklington as a pilot officer in May 1940 and during the Battle of Britain he shot down five enemy aircraft, shared in the destruction of another, and damaged two additional aircraft. He was awarded the DFC on 7 January 1941. The RAF tunic pictured here was worn by Williams during the Battle of Britain period, before his promotion to flying officer in April 1941. It was custom tailored by J. E. Carhart Ltd of Stoke-on-Trent. Williams was given temporary command of No. 121 (Eagle) Squadron in August 1942 and led this force of American fighter pilots flying for the RAF until their transition over to the US Army Air Force in September 1942. Williams later commanded No. 615 Squadron in India and retired from the RAF as Squadron Leader in 1945.

ALL IST

KAPOOT!

R.I.P.
TUNNEL
#58

WELCOME

to

POW

camp

BARTH · GERMANY

Kriegsgefangenenpost

Mit Luftpost
Par Avion

GEPRÜFT
31

REVISED BY AUTHORITY OF
THE DISTRICT POSTAL CENSOR

Empfangsort:
Straße:
Land: U.S.A.

Gebührenfrei!

EXAMINED BY CENSOR 274

PRISONERS OF WAR

During the Second World War, more than ten thousand airmen became prisoners of war (POWs). After bailing out of a disabled aircraft over enemy territory, pilots and aircrew had little time to escape from roving enemy patrols searching for downed airmen. Air Commodore Charles Clarke, who served as a bomber pilot during the war, landed in a snowdrift after abandoning his Lancaster bomber and was immediately captured by German soldiers. He was sent to Stalag Luft III prison camp, where he was forbidden to speak to any other prisoners and had difficulties finding other RAF airmen. At one point, he began singing a tune from a popular movie he had seen in London earlier that week and was pleased to hear another POW answer in kind – his first indication that he was not alone in the camp.

RAF crewman Andrew Wiseman was captured after his Halifax bomber was disabled. He parachuted into France, where he was picked up. Wiseman was Jewish, but the RAF identification tags issued to him indicated a different religious affiliation. Wiseman had tried to correct the error but when he discovered how difficult a process it would be decided to keep the set he had. The decision may have saved his life.

This model of the bunk used by a Polish RAF POW was made out of scrap materials during his incarceration in a German camp. Also shown are POW identification tags issued to prisoners (bottom right), censored POW mail (bottom left), RAF wings made of bone (upper centre), and two books published by POWs at Stalag I (right). Stalags were used to house NCO ranks while a separate camp, called an Oflag, was used for officers.

BATTLE OF BRITAIN MEDAL GROUPING

RAF airmen that participated in the Battle of Britain were entitled to special recognition. Only 2,917 of those who became known to history as 'The Few' were permitted to wear a special clasp on the 1939–45 Star medal that signified their service during Britain's critical time. In addition, aircrew were presented with a silver gilt rosette that was sewn onto the ribbon for the 1939–45 Star to denote their service. Only those who flew at least one operational mission during the established Battle of Britain timeframe of 10 July to 31 October 1940 were eligible to receive the clasp and rosette.

The medal grouping shown here (lower right) – consisting of (from left) the 1939–45 Star; Aircrew Europe Star; Defence Medal; and 1939–45 War Medal – belonged to Pilot Officer Gordon Eric Ellis (pictured, top left). He joined the RAF on a short service commission in February 1939 and was attached to No. 6 Operational Training Unit at Sutton Bridge from No. 229 Squadron in early July 1940. He made this transition to convert to Hurricanes and was transferred to No. 64 Squadron quickly (20 July 1940). Ellis is credited with shooting down one German fighter during the Battle of Britain but was discharged in early 1941 due to injuries suffered in a crash landing on 8 August 1940. The King's Badge (top right), which was authorised by the Ministry of Pensions, was also presented to Ellis. The badge was to be worn in the buttonhole of civilian dress, lest a disabled soldier be mistaken for one who had shirked his duty during wartime.

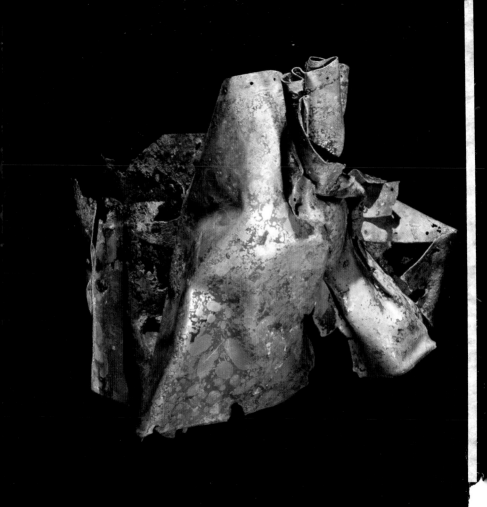

IN MEMORIAM

The cost of the RAF's experience in the Second World War was high. During the war, the RAF attained strength of more than 1.2 million men and women. Of this number, about seventy thousand RAF personnel were lost. Of the nearly three thousand aircrew that participated in the Battle of Britain, 544 lost their lives in the battle and a further 814 died before the end of the war.

The Battle of Britain monument records the names of the 2,936 flyers from fifteen nations who flew in the battle. One of these was Malcolm Ravenhill, who joined the RAF in 1938. He flew Hurricanes with No. 229 Squadron until shot down on 1 September 1940. After recovering from shock at Shorncliffe Hospital, he returned to his squadron and resumed combat operations until shot down again and killed on 30 September in the crash of Hurricane P2815 near Ightham. He was twenty-seven years old. The crash site was excavated in the mid-1980s and relics removed for museum display. This photograph of the twisted wreckage of Ravenhill's plane serves as mute testimony to his loss. Winston Churchill said:

> The gratitude of every home in our island, in our Empire and indeed throughout the world, except in the abodes of the guilty, goes out to the British airmen, who, undaunted by odds, unwearied in their constant challenge and mortal danger, are turning the tide of the world war by their prowess and devotion. Never in the field of human conflict was so much owed by so many to so few.

BIBLIOGRAPHY

Allen, H. R. 'Dizzy'. *Battle for Britain: The Recollections of Wing Commander H. R. 'Dizzy' Allen, DFC*. Arthur Barker Ltd., 1973.

Barber, Mark. *RAF Fighter Command: The Western Front 1939–42*. Osprey Publishing Ltd., 2012.

Campion, Garry. *The Good Fight: Battle of Britain Propaganda and The Few*. Palgrave Macmillan, 2009.

Charlwood, Don. *No Moon Tonight*. Angus & Robertson, 1956.

Cormack, Andrew. *The Royal Air Force 1939–45*. Osprey Publishing, 1990.

Francis, Martin. *The Flyer: British Culture and the Royal Air Force 1939–45*. Oxford University Press, 2008.

Gelb, Norman. *Scramble: A Narrative History of the Battle of Britain*. Harcourt Brace Jovanovich, 1985.

Hobart, Malcolm C. *Badges & Uniforms of the Royal Air Force*. Pen & Sword, 2012.

Kaplan, Philip and Collier, Richard. *The Few*. Blandford Press, 1989.

Kingcome, Brian. *A Willingness to Die*. Tempus, 1999.

Largent, Willard. *RAF Wings Over Florida: Memories of British Air Cadets*. Purdue University Press, 2000.

Manchester, William. 'Undaunted by Odds', *MHQ: The Quarterly Journal of Military History*, spring 1998.

Pateman, Colin. *Goldfish, Caterpillars & Guinea Pigs*. Fonthill, 2012.

Prodger, Mick J. *Luftwaffe vs. RAF: Flying Clothing of the Air War, 1939–45*. Schiffer Military History, 1997.

_____. *Luftwaffe vs. RAF: Flying Equipment of the Air War, 1939–45*. Schiffer Military History, 1998.

Wynn, Kenneth G. *Men of the Battle of Britain*. CCB Associates, 1999.

INDEX